Did You Count Your Money?

By Santo
Published by **ReeSaa Pvt. Ltd.**

All rights reserved. No part of this book may be reproduced, stored in a retrieval system, communicated or transmitted in any form or by any means without written permission.

All enquiries can be addressed to reesaa@indiavivid.com

Disclaimer: This book is based on personal experience of the author and should not be construed as a financial guide or plan. The author cannot be held responsible/liable for any loses or financial impact because of any ideas/thoughts shared in this book. Readers are advised independent financial advice to assess their individual situation.

Visit reesaa.com
Copyright 2017 @ ReeSaa Pvt. Ltd. All Rights Reserved

Why I Wrote This Book?

The opportunity to help and guide you through my learnings of over 8 years, inspired me to pen my thoughts in the form of this book. I wanted to pass on my insights in a short and simplistic manner to provide you with the ability to be in control of your finances and money.

I have aspired to capture what I have learnt through the years as a guide to help with measures, metrics and principles to be better in control of the your own personal financial situation.

-**Santo**

Please share your thoughts and ideas at reesaa@indiavivid.com. If you have ideas that you think should be included in this book, I would love to hear.

Preface

I didn't really understand money until I was into ten years of my working life. Money was till then an income through a singular means - employment. I didn't know how much money I had (apart from seeing my bank balance from time to time) and didn't really know what was happening with the money I had.

Early in 2009, I decided to capture my world around money in a spreadsheet to essentially understand "where I stood" with my money. So the **journey of counting my money** began.

This book shares that learning with you in a simplistic way to give you a basic idea and a tool to know

- where you stand in the continuum of personal finance wrt. your wealth and money
- help you gauge where you are headed wrt.

- leave you thoughts around where you want to be in the wealth continuum

with the basic premise that:

> *"You will never where you are headed unless you know where you stand, unless you know where you want to go and unless you have an action plan to take you there."*

In this book, I have tried to avoid jargons and financial language which makes it difficult for a layman to really understand where he is at with his money.

Happy Reading.

About the Author

Santo is going through life just as you and me with lots of questions and few answers here and there. With an MBA in Finance and a desire to make a difference in people's life, Santo is a part author, part technologist and an aspirant for making a difference to your life.

Santo runs IndiaVivid as its Founder with a goal to 'discovering, sharing and celebrating India" as a passion. As a Founder & Director of ReeSaa Pvt. Ltd, Santo also endeavors to making a difference to children's life through its "Dia Stories" for children (books.indiavivid.com)

Santo can be reached at reesaa@indiavivid.com or via reesaa.com

In this book, Santo has captured his learning through his growth as an individual, through his education in a top management college and also the learnings and feedback loop generated through the course of his working life.

Acknowledgements

For **My Dad** who always inspired me to believe in myself and for teaching me to follow the goals with sincerity

For **My Mom** who taught me the meaning of love

For **my children** who present me with a smile and give the courage to go on day after day.

And for **my wife**, the reason I could write this book.

Table of Contents

Where am I standing?..9
Am I Making Progress? 14
What Am I Worth? 18
Am I Doing The Right Thing?................................26
What Is My Money Doing For Me? 32

Where am I standing?

In 2009, I started creating a simple framework for myself to start capturing little bits of information to gather an understanding of my balance position wrt. to money (of whatever little I had) across different buckets.

When I say buckets, I mean elements such as your cash position, fixed deposits, real estate market value.

This initial framework helped me a lot in understanding where I stood, how much money I had. It essentially provided a snapshot of my balance across different buckets as I like to call it. **I had taken Step 1 in counting my money.**

So what did I do?

I started off with capturing some basic information classified into different buckets such as:

Bank Account	Location	Account Balance in AUD	Account Balance in USD

Why in USD? - I like to believe that USD is the de-facto global currency and will continue to be so for the distant future and its useful to track against it.

I used the above simple methodology to capture information across

- balances by family member either single or joint

- classified across buckets such as

    - Savings

        - Liquid and Cash

        - Fixed Deposit

        - Rental Bond

- Retirement Accounts
    - Superannuation/401K
- Investments
    - Mutual Funds
    - Shares
- Loan Balance such as
    - Home Loan
    - Educational Loan
    - Car Loans
    - Credit Card Balance

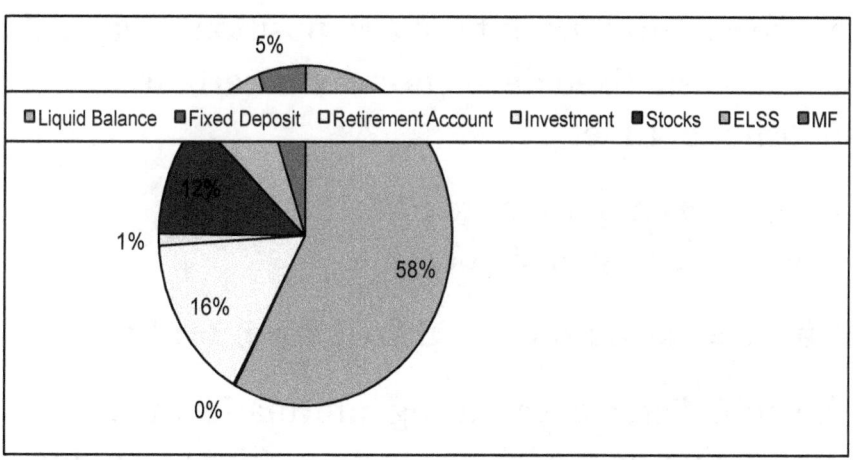

You can easily expand this list to cater for any other money buckets that you can think of or having either **money owing** or **with you**.

To begin with the above information captured gave a great basis to understand where did my money lie. It was an important step in understanding and knowing my "**Balance of Position**". The picture here is a sample representation of a balance of position as a percentage in a pie chart format. This

is perhaps a classic example of how the distribution shouldn't be.

Summary:

Balance of Position for me was nothing but a stated position of value such as cash, fixed deposits etc on a certain snapshot of time.

Here, it was important to understand the importance of snapshot of time.

Why was snapshot of time important?

This initial step of capturing information had essentially provided me a starting point at a point of time providing me a view of my balance position across different financial elements.

And the most important thing was (which I would later realize) that it gave me a sense of direction of where I was headed with my money as I started plotting my position over time - we will discuss this later in subsequent chapter.

Why don't you try?

If you are like me when I was in 2009, why don't' you try and get a feel of your balance of position. It might give you a sense of strength in what you are doing or provide a view to what you should be doing.

Note: It is important to capture other elements of finance that impacts a family including Insurance taken, Superannuation/401K balance, Loan Balances, Market Price of Properties you own etc. This gives a complete picture and also helps you keep a tab of your financial well being. You might find it easier to go through it with your better half from time to time - helps both of you align to a singular goal.

Am I Making Progress?

The initiative that I had taken in 2009 to list down my balance position had helped in gaining a great deal of understanding of what I was doing right and what I was doing wrong.

For example, I realized that 58% of my balance was in Savings Account which yielded next to nothing. Essentially, my money was doing nothing for me.

And this led me to take the next step in enhancing the information that I captured. I wanted to know what was happening with the balance of those amounts over time. This stemmed from the interest to understand whether I was taking the right steps based on the insights that I had got from my financial position as also to understand what my trend looked like.

I wanted to know whether I was **"Making Progress?"**

I spent the next couple of years capturing the same information that I had captured in 2009 while adding two bits of additional information to it:

- **Time dimension:** While I captured the balance of my positions every quarterly, I maintained January as the base for comparison: Jan-09 to Jan-10 to Jan-11. It gave a perspective of what was happening to my money and finances.

- **Growth dimension:** Another important metric that I added was the cumulative growth to give a cumulative differential year-on-year. This gave me a perspective of the increase in the balance of my position between the intervening period. Now, I knew by how much my savings balance had increased from Jan-09 to Jan-10 to Jan-11 on a yearly basis.

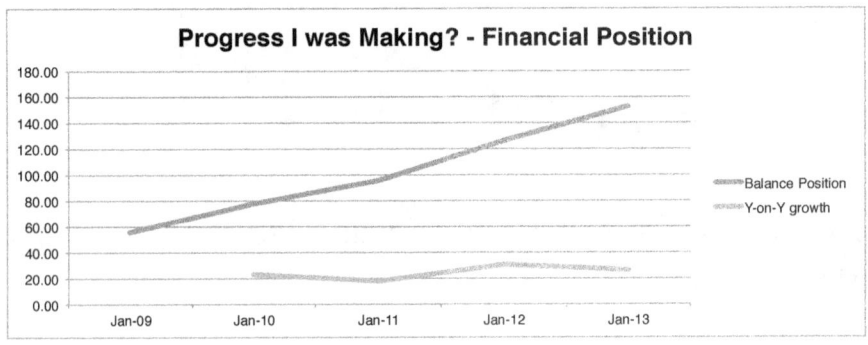

The figure above is for representational purpose but is an excellent example of what I saw happening for me. I had essence created a view to help me with and gave me a greater understanding of where I stood at a point of time in terms of finance and money.

For You:

Quiet often we are tied up in expenses through credit card, loans and via other means which can quickly spiral out of control. I suggest you create the above and a get a view of the year-on-year growth. You could start of with a quarter on quarter view moving on to a year-on-year.

It is essential to not over spend your time doing this. Its more of a guide for you to be able to make decisions. If you are not adding anything to your financial position y-on-y, you better re-think your strategy now.

What Am I Worth?

I had been tracking my balances and marking the trends year on year. I was also aware of the delta changes year over year. Somewhere in 2015, I realized that although I knew my balances, it didn't really give a true picture of **"What My Networth"** really was? I had no idea whether overall I was in a better financial position and whether I **owed** more than I **owned**.

This is when I added another dimension to the information that I was capturing. I started capturing the type of the balance in question as also whether it was an **Asset** or a **Liability**.

Bank Account	Location	Type of Account	Asset/ Liability	Account Balance in AUD	Account Balance in USD

Essentially what I started to do was to create what companies do which is called the **"Balance**

Sheet". This was my **"Personal Balance Sheet** and created in a simplistic manner without the need for understanding the complicated accounting that goes with Finance.

I referred the type of account to classify it as an Asset or a Liability to determine my **"Personal Networth"**.

Basic Concepts Explained

Let me quickly touch base upon some of the terms I introduced here so that it doesn't sound complicated to you and you are able to follow through what I really did.

Asset:

I classified everything I own of significance as an **Asset**. Examples of Assets included

- Cash
- Investments
- Property
- Cars etc..

Liabilities

Anything that I owed in debts, I classified them as **Liabilities.** Examples included

- Home Loan
- Education Loan
- Rental deposit I maintained with me for properties that I rented out etc..

My Personal Networth was = "Assets - Liabilities". It was everything I owned - everything I owed

And my balance sheet was nothing but a representation of my balance position of assets and liabilities at a point of time. I had put the assets together while I bucketed my liabilities separately below it. And I used the formula I mentioned above to calculate my personal networth.

In addition to the above, I did few things differently as well. I knowingly classified Property separately as well to have a representation as below:

MY PORTFOLIO BUCKET			
Portfolio	Balance of Position	Target % Income Yearly	Target Income Yearly in USD
Shares			
Mutual Funds			
Fixed Deposits			
Bonds and so on.			
Property			

ASSETS		
Asset Bucket	Current Balance	Delta Change since Jan this year
Savings		
Fixed Deposit		
Shares		
etc..		

As I had mentioned above I always measured against Jan 1st. It fell within the December holiday time period, I got time to review my position during that time and also helped me in personal planning for the next year.

I had similar representations for Property bucket and Liabilities as shown below:

ASSETS - PROPERTY		
Property Bucket	Current Market Value	Delta Change since Jan this year
Property A		
Property B		
etc..		

LIABILITIES		
Liability Bucket	Outstanding Value	Delta Change since Jan this year
Loan		
Rental Bond		
etc..		

Note: I always calculated 90% of current market value (based on recent sales in the area) for networth purposes to take care of real estate commission and any negative surprises.

Because of the way I had started capturing my financial information and money position, there are 2 additional bits of information that I leveraged based on what I had been capturing since 2009:

- I had a snapshot of my Assets and Liabilities and in effect networth on Jan 1 every year since 2009. I was able to build this based on the data captured earlier through a simple excel worksheet.

- I had a view of the delta changes year on year based on my personal balance sheet position as on 1st Jan every year.

As shown in the chart of my liability position, there was a spike in Jan-14 owing to a new home loan. There were also periods of time when my liability position reduced (change was -ve) as I paid some amount of my loans.

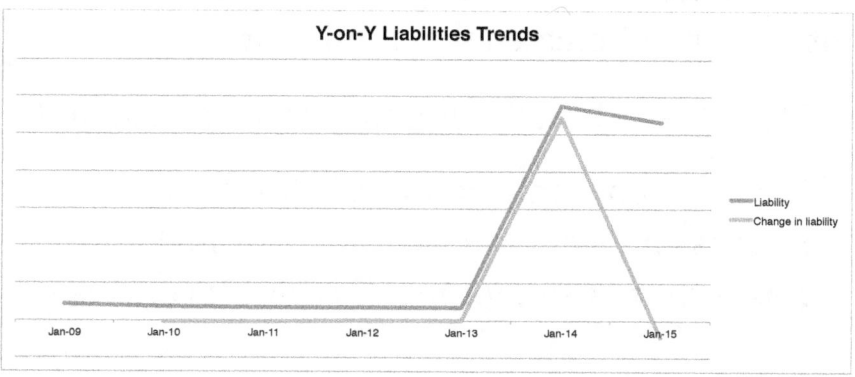

As shown in the adjoining chart you can create your trends and charts using the data that you have gathered to provide ways to analyze and understand your financial position in a very simplistic way.

An important concept that I saw for myself was the concept of **"Money making Money"** as is evident from the networth trend. As the networth

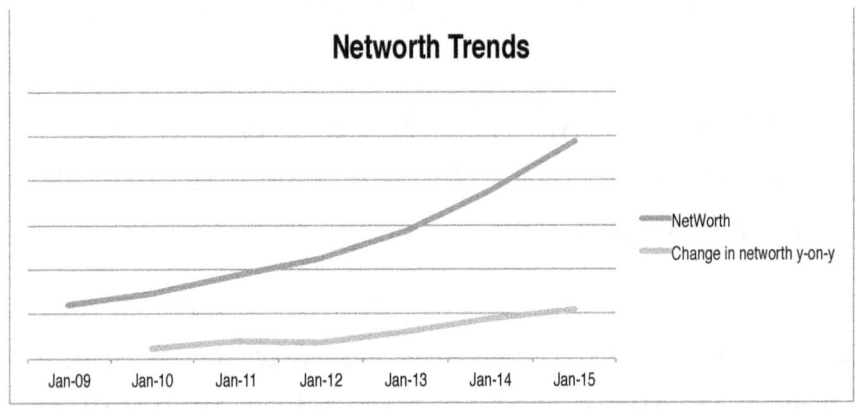

increases, your money can be a potential money earner if you are able to make the best use of it as you see here. There are 2 important things I noticed when I created the trend chart:

1. My net-worth was increasing year-on-year and

2. Income from some of it was helping me increase my networth year-on-year making **passive income** for me. (Passive Income is

income generated through revenue streams requiring minimal or no effort).

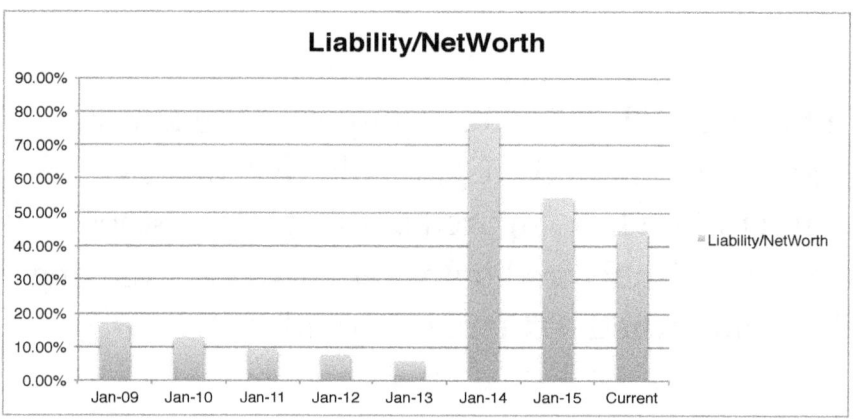

Another metric you can generate with data so captured is the **Liability/NetWorth.** It gives a very good view of how much you owe versus how much you am worth. This prevents you from getting overboard with taking too much liability upon yourself.

Am I Doing The Right Thing?

In finance and as in life, its important to know whether we are in the right path. In previous chapters, you have figured out where you stood. You have also figured out whether you are moving ahead and whether there is a trend to it.

I had been measuring my net worth, assets and liabilities year on year till 2016. It gave me a perspective but didn't really tell me whether I was doing the right thing. It didn't tell me how much liabilities were good. I didn't have a benchmark to measure myself against.

This is when I added few metrics to my calculation. I call this my **"Personal Ratios"**.

MY PERSONAL RATIOS

Metrics	Definition	Additional description	Bench mark	Classification
Liquidity Ratio	Liquid Assets/ Net Worth	This is the amount of money that can be deployed/withdrawn at short notice versus your net worth for emergency purposes. Liquid Assets are those that can be converted into cash in quick time	> 15%	Liquidity
Idle Cash Ratio	Cash balance in savings account etc../take home pay	Idle cash ratio should be looked at in conjunction with the above. You need to have liquid money for a rainy day without having too much lying somewhere without adding too much to your income	< 20%	Liquidity

MY PERSONAL RATIOS

Metrics	Definition	Additional description	Bench mark	Classification
Total Debt to Asset Ratio	Total Liabilities/ Total Assets	Ratio of liability to your total assets (not net worth)	< 50%	Serviceability of Debt
Total Debt to Net Worth	Total Outstanding Loans/ Net Worth	Ration of liability to your total net worth	< 0.8	Serviceability of Debt
Total Debt to Income Ratio	Total Annual Debt Payments/ Total Annual take home salary	This provides serviceability of loan (ability to service any loan through your income)	<45%	Serviceability of Debt
Solvency Ratio	Total Networth/ Total Assets	This is another metric providing ability to service your debt	> = 50%	Serviceability of Debt

MY PERSONAL RATIOS				
Metrics	Definition	Additional description	Bench mark	Classification
Life Insurance Coverage Ratio	Life Cover/ Total Post Tax Annual Income	Insurance is a key financial planning element that we should all look at. This provides a view of life insurance coverage that we should to cover our family in case of unforeseen circumstances. It refer to Term Life Insurance (TPD + Death)	> 7%	Insurance Coverage
Net Invested Assets to Net Worth	Total Assets under Investment/Total Net Worth	A key aspects of financial planning is to let your investments generate money for you. This metric provides a view of the assets which are under investment.	> = 50%	Investment

MY PERSONAL RATIOS

Metrics	Definition	Additional description	Bench mark	Classification
Savings Ratio	Savings/ Gross Income	How much your income is going back into increasing your net worth	> 20%	Income Generation Ability
Wealth Ratio	(Passive + Portfolio + Interest Income) / Total Expenses	Cash flow that is being generated through passive means (without your direct involvement)	> 1	Income Generation Ability
Non-mortgage debt to Income Ratio	Total Annual non-mortgage debt payment/ total annual take home pay		< 15%	Debt Serviceability

Once I finished the above calculations to measure my personal ratios, I quickly realized that my liquidity ratio was 40%, i.e. I wasn't leveraging my money very well with most sitting idle as cash.

I wasn't doing the right thing after all. My Life Insurance Coverage was around 2%.

My Idle Cash ratio was huge being 183%.

Using the personal ratios for your personal situation is a sure shot way to get a grip of your personal financial situation. It helps to understand whether you are doing the right thing, and if not gives you indication of what needs to be done.

What Is My Money Doing For Me?

In trying to assess whether I was doing the right thing, I had unearthed another important element of financial planning. I still did not know what my money was doing for me.

The "Idle Cash Ratio" and "Liquidity Ratio" was an indication that I had cash sitting idle for me doing nothing. In addition I also came to realize that I was far away from realizing the dream of having a Wealth Ratio of 1.

Where do I want to be?

My financial goal was now clear as a metric and I had means to measure how far I was from it. I wanted to be financially free, i.e. I wanted my income from sources such as passive income, interest income and my portfolio buckets greater than my expenses. I essentially wanted my

Wealth Ratio As 1.

And for me to move towards my goal, I had to better utilize what I had with me. It was important for me to know what my money was doing for me.

I had been capturing my balance of position across different elements (portfolio buckets) such as Investments, Savings, Superannuation, Shares, Mutual Funds, Loan etc..I realized that I wasn't really making the best possible use of my different financial buckets in terms of generating income for me. I wasn't aware of my Cash flow situation across each of these elements year on year. I was also heavily dependent on a single source for my cash flow (my employment - not a good position to be in).

I was able to use my learnings to craft a view of how much income I wanted from each of these portfolio classes and went back to the drawing board to focus on how to achieve that.

I had created a view as follows:

I was on my way to reaching financial freedom. Hopefully soon :). And hoping you are able to leverage this learning to join me on the way to being financially free.

Do share your learnings similar to mine with us at **reesaa@indiavivid.com** *and visit* **reesaa.com** *to share your thoughts.*

www.ingramcontent.com/pod-product-compliance
Lightning Source LLC
Chambersburg PA
CBHW061452180526
45170CB00004B/1676